2022 Written
Mike Hinton's
sister Patty & niece Debbie

PRAISING STORMS

PRAISING STORMS

Through Faith, Hope and Love

Patricia Markus
Debbie Leuzzi

Columbus, Ohio

Praising Storms: Through Faith, Hope and Love

Published by Gatekeeper Press
2167 Stringtown Rd, Suite 109
Columbus, OH 43123-2989
www.GatekeeperPress.com

Library of Congress Control Number: 2021945342

ISBN (paperback): 9781662912504
eISBN: 9781662912726

Dedication

Dedicated to my beautiful daughter Megan, who is a living testament to God's presence and the power of faith, hope, and the greatest of all love. To God who called me to share my family's storms according to Romans 10:17 (The Message):

"But how can people call for help if they don't know who to trust? And how can they know who to trust if they haven't heard of the One who can be trusted? And how can they hear if nobody tells them? And how is anyone going to tell them, unless someone is sent to do it?"

Thank you, Lord, for choosing us to share our story and your love with others.

Pat and Megan

Table of Contents

Preface

> God is always present with us. When we put our faith in Jesus, God gives us his Spirit, who dwells with us and in us.
>
> (John 14:16-17 NIV)

Have you ever experienced a real phenomenon? Something more than mere coincidence. Maybe an uncanny encounter that seemed too good to be true. Or maybe ... someone, or something showing up, out-of-the-blue, just when you needed it most. I've heard these incidents referred to as kismet, fate, God winks, and more. I call them God kisses. I believe these heavenly placed gifts are an expression of the Lord's love for us. The Holy Spirit is God dwelling in us and His promise of hope to us. He is our helper, our comforter, our guide, our strength. He often materializes in remarkable ways, through wonderful people and unforgettable experiences. Each incident of

God's divine intervention renewed my spirit, guided my direction, and fueled my energy to swim through the floods that threatened to drown me. I've learned that the more I remain open to the presence of the Holy Spirit, the more He intervenes.

Through my tumultuous journey, I've been asked by my family and friends to share my story. When I think back to the day that shattered my world – I'm reminded of that first encounter with Jesus. It was in that cold, dank hospital bathroom, where he kissed my tears away. As I stood basking in His warmth, I found the strength to move forward. He told me it was just the beginning of a long struggle, and I should be writing my story down. Documenting the daily battles and how I would witness Him working all things together for good. Over the years, I wanted to do as God asked me to do – I really did. I continue to hear His whispers calling to me, but the timing was never right, and the days turned to years.

It was in the spring of 2019 when I felt God leading me to invite my niece, Debbie, to a Word of Life conference. Debbie lives in another state, and I didn't want her to feel any pressure to join me, but I did feel a strong push to invite her. The second I mentioned it to her, there was not a moment of hesitation. I was taken aback when she responded, "Absolutely, I need something like this now more than ever." There were significant hardships happening in our extended family, and I felt we needed to draw closer to the Lord to face what was waiting ahead. Ironically, just a year before, she and I had talked about writing that book - together. God was still prompting me with his voice to share my testimonies. But once again, the days of our lives got in the way and more storms were to be weathered.

When I showed up at this conference, I could barely walk. My overall health had suffered too many blows. My niece was extremely worried and concerned about my physical state. As we settled in for the first session, Paula Dunn—the speaker and musician for the weekend—talked about the time God had led her to a similar conference. She said that throughout the conference He was calling her to write a book - something she never thought of doing. Debbie and I immediately looked at each other and just grinned from ear to ear. God had brought us together to hear this message - truly a divine encounter. I felt so much better, physically, and spiritually. I was exhilarated at the thought of us working together fulfilling God's calling. I noticed Debbie hastily jotting down notes. She nudged me to look at her notes where she had circled what she believed could be the name of the book - Praising Storms. I loved it!

Following the conference, we set up a schedule to meet by phone on a regular basis to move God's plan forward. He showered us with multiple hugs and kisses throughout this journey. We were consistently blown away when one of us would speak of an idea and the other one had been simultaneously thinking about the same thing. While writing this book, the storms continued raging through the lives of our family and friends. It was tough going for both of us. And yet, through it all, God continued to remind us that He was always there every step of the way. Each chapter ended up ministering to us and those around us. It also deepened our relationships with God, family, friends, and each other. I pray you find peace in knowing that when God takes you through turbulent waters - it's because the devil can't swim.

> "May the God of hope fill you with all joy and peace as you trust in him, so that you may overflow with hope by the power of the Holy Spirit."
>
> (Romans 15:13)

Pat and Debbie

Stripes Through Storms

> "'Do not fear, for I have redeemed you; I have summoned you by name; you are mine. When you pass through the waters, I will be with you; and when you pass through the rivers, they will not sweep over you. When you walk through the fire, you will not be burned; the flames will not set you ablaze.'"
>
> (Isaiah 43:1-2)

A storm happens when there is a disturbance of the normal condition of the atmosphere, manifesting itself by winds of unusual force or direction. These are often accompanied by a heavy rainfall, and a violent outbreak of thunder and lightning. Storms come in all shapes and sizes. Sometimes we can prepare for them, and sometimes they just stir up out of nowhere. I find it fascinating that on a bright day you can be out driving and suddenly have a storm kick up that is so torrential - it's immobilizing. And yet, a few miles later- the roads are clear, and the sun is shining. Much like life – one minute your day seems bright and full of joy, and in the blink of an eye a storm thunders in and blasts your world into utter darkness.

The collateral damage from most storms is minimal – an inconvenience, a minor setback. But then, there comes a storm that rages through with such fury it destroys everything in its path. I can't possibly describe the agony that one endures when weathering a life-changing storm. A friend once shared an analogy of what it means to them to survive trauma. She said, "It's like we all start out our existence as horses. When we battle through a thrashing storm that leaves us permanently scarred – we become zebras. The stripes separate the zebras from horses. Once you have the stripes, you can never go back to being a horse." I vividly remember the instant I became a zebra. The power of that storm was so intense that I could feel its eye burning a hole through my heart. Its gale-force winds shook every fiber of my soul, and the lightning that struck being so profound that I knew I would never see the world the same again. There was no turning back, this storm permanently striped my skin.

The storms continued but the Lord, my savior helped me find the silver lining in each one. The indescribable closeness I experienced with Him in quiet times of prayer and devotion. Finding shelter and comfort in in His wings during times of worship and praise. Whether it was His loving presence, or the Holy Spirit inside of me, He never failed. Trusting in God's promise to provide the grace and mercy I need to navigate any storm gave me the supernatural strength to continue moving forward. To shift from a place of severe physical and emotional pain to a place of joy, hope and peace. Just like the beautiful rainbow that follow a storm, God's presence filled me with His radiant light. He would bless me with moments of happiness when I thought I'd never smile again.

If God came to me in advance of my storms and revealed the amazing goodness - the silver lining - and asked me if I was ready to go - I would have said NO WAY! Even if He had shown me the incredible outcome of many lives being transformed along the way, I would've still said no. But He didn't ask me and I'm grateful that He didn't. I would have missed so many blessings - so many miracles. Ultimately in life, our purpose is to be the hands and feet of Jesus and through our actions, bring heaven to earth. We are sent for others, not for ourselves. We are here to shoulder burdens and tough times, so we are prepared to comfort and carry each other through life's hardships. A popular adage is, "God will only give you what you can handle." I do not believe that. If He only gave me what I could handle - what would I need him for? I discovered that when I needed Him most - I was able to surrender it. To let go and let God. He didn't just change my circumstance; He changed me.

> "God is our refuge and strength, an ever-present help in trouble.[2] Therefore we will not fear, though the earth gives way, and the mountains fall into the heart of the sea,[3] though its waters roar and foam and the mountains quake with their surging."
>
> [Psalm 46:1-3]

Pre-Accident Pat's Family
(Boz, Megan, Pat, Kelly)

Meditate on God's Truth and Words:

Surrendering – letting go and letting God - sounds easy in theory but can be difficult in practice. Keeping our eyes on the Lord is a daily discipline and requires a great deal of prayer and reflection. I've provided space at the end of each chapter to meditate on God's word, to praise Him through a worship song, and I've offered questions to ponder. Ultimately, through the reflection of your own experiences, my hope is that a better understanding of God's purpose and plan for your life becomes clearer.

- Capture the message you think God wants you to hear from this chapter.
- Meditation Verse: Read and meditate on the following verse and reflect on how this applies to your everyday life. Pick out one word that stands out most to you when you read the following verse.
    - *"'For I know the plans I have for you,' declares the Lord, 'plans to prosper you and not to harm you, plans to give you hope and a future.'" (Jeremiah 29:11)*
- Praise Song: Search for the following worship song and listen to it. When you're done, reflect on what you heard and how it made you feel.
    - "Praise You in This Storm" by Casting Crowns
- Reflect on the following questions:
    - What do you need from God to calm the storms that may sweep through your life?

- How has God's presence shown up in the middle of your storms?
- What support do you need to help shoulder the weight of your own burdens?
- Based on the burdens you have shouldered, what opportunities exist for you to help others?

The Storm That Rocked My World

> "Then he got into the boat and his disciples followed him. Suddenly a furious storm came up on the lake, so that the waves swept over the boat. But Jesus was sleeping. The disciples went and woke him, saying, 'Lord, save us! We're going to drown!' He replied, 'You of little faith, why are you so afraid?' Then he got up and rebuked the winds and the waves, and it was completely calm. The men were amazed and asked, 'What kind of man is this? Even the winds and the waves obey him!"
>
> (Matthew 8:23-27)

Let me start at the beginning when an accident changed my family's life - forever - in an instant. It was Friday, November 15, 1996, at 12:15 p.m. I was teaching at a city district school in Rochester, NY, and was on my break.

Suddenly an extremely uncomfortable feeling came over me, a real and scary sense of dread. I turned to my coworker and said, "There is a huge black cloud here and it scares me, and I know that either you or me, or both of us, will not return to work on Monday." As it turned out, I would not return to work for an awfully long time. Looking back on that moment, if I had been where I am now, I would have fallen to my knees and prayed my heart out, but I wasn't in that place and just shook off that feeling of dread and returned to my classroom.

Just as classes were changing, the school's social worker came and said I had an urgent phone call in the office and that I needed to come immediately. I quickly settled my class and followed her. As I walked down the hallway, I knew that I was about to receive bad news. I thought it was going to be about my mother who had been ill, but instead it was my husband on the phone. With a shaky and scared voice, he told me my oldest daughter had been in a serious car accident and I needed to get to the hospital ASAP. I remember screaming, "No! Not my Megan." My husband says the only thing he remembers of that day was my scream.

After placing down the phone, the office spun around me, and things became surreal. People came from their offices and were looking at me with concern. As I started to cry, their eyes turned down. My emotional state was intense—a sense of helplessness filled the room. The office secretary then stepped forward and wrapped me in her arms and uttered soothing words as she led me towards

the Sovereign Lord comes escape from death." And with that surrendering plea, I felt God's peace wash over me. I knew He was with us, and he had heard my prayer. As people were shedding their emotions in many ways, the all too familiar question of "Why do bad things happen to good people" was on everyone's mind, especially mine. My Megan, seventeen about to be eighteen, was so healthy, vibrant, determined, and ready to take on the world. "Why, why, why Lord?" was screaming in my mind.

When I was finally able to see Megan, after eight hours of agonizing waiting, I entered her room and was bombarded by the buzzers and beepers and people running about tending to her needs. I was amazed that with the extent of her injuries, she had not a visible scratch on her. So many times, I was grateful she was saved from horrible scars, and other times I struggled with how her injuries could be so life changing when I could not see them. It says in Hebrews 11:1 (KJV) that "Faith is the substance of things hoped for, the evidence of things not seen." That is much like my struggle with faith, believing in what I do not see and trusting God to guide me.

After I saw Megan for the first time, I became physically ill and ran to the bathroom. The first few times I was with a family member or friend making sure I was okay, but the last time I went alone. I felt like I was in a movie. I pounded my fist on the wall and screamed out over-and-over again, "Why? Why, my Megan?" Now this may be hard to believe but I am telling you, God came to me in that cold, dimly lit bathroom. I was facing the wall and began feeling an intense heat. I felt a presence of brilliant and warm light. Without audible words or sounds, I heard God say, "Look for the blessings, speak to many, and be prepared to write." The light and warmth faded after receiving his message. Despite the trauma and information that I had to absorb on that day, and the time that has passed since, the experience was so extreme that it put a divine imprint on my faith journey for life. With the Holy Spirit working through me as a vessel for hope, I have now shared Megan's stories with groups of people, large and small, young and old, believers and people who God is still working on their hearts.

After many years, I have stopped grieving for what we lost. There is a reason Megan survived. Despite the daily hardship of caring for a child that is unable to functionally do anything, I praise God for sparing her. I believe that the Lord provides us with the grace we need to get through each day and on that day, it would have killed me to lose my daughter. Let's face it. We all have storms in our lives with different circumstances and magnitudes. Each of these storms have the power to alter our path. It is through these times that the Lord wants us to call out to him. He is there—right by our side—never forsaking us. God provides us the freedom to try and control things on our own. But through him, the Lord can transform us from the inside out and move us from powerless to powerful. Through the sharing of my family's story, it is my hope that God's goodness is revealed and brings a spirit of hope and trust that the Lord's grace is sufficient. He provides us with what we need to weather the storms of life.

> "Even though I walk through the darkest valley, I will fear no evil, for you are with me; your rod and your staff, they comfort me."
>
> (Psalm 23:4)

Meditate on God's Truth and Words:

- Capture the message you think God wants you to hear from this chapter.
- Meditation Verse: Read and meditate on the following verse and reflect on how this applies to your everyday life. Pick out one word that stands out most to you when you read the following verse.
  - "He stilled the storm to a whisper; the waves of the sea were hushed." (Psalm 107:29)
- Praise Song: Search for the following worship song and listen to it. When you're done, reflect on what you heard and how it made you feel.
  - "Rescue Story" by Zach Williams
- Reflect on the following questions:
  - In what ways have you felt the presence of God during life's storms?
  - How has the Lord brought you peace during your journey through these storms?
  - In what ways has God provided for your needs, or made good out of bad, through the storms of life?

I Will Lift My Eyes...

"I lift my eyes to the mountains—where does my help come from? My help comes from the Lord the Maker of heaven and earth. He will not let your foot slip—he who watches over you will not slumber; indeed, he who watches over Israel will neither slumber nor sleep. The Lord watches over you—the Lord is your shade at your right hand; the sun will not harm you by day, nor the moon by night. The Lord will keep you from all harm—he will watch over your life; the Lord will watch over your coming and going both now and forevermore."

(Psalm 121:1-8)

Oh, how that Scripture settles my soul. Repeatedly, from one crisis moment to the next, God's spirit led me to a place of rest and peace through his words and grace. I remember the first time the Lord whispered to me this verse. Megan had come out of the coma early following the accident, but the extent of her brain injuries left her with little to no functional abilities. With Megan no longer needing intensive medical care, she was moved to a local rehab facility for continued rehabilitation. Although I had an army of support to relieve me, it was agonizing for me to leave her side. But my other daughter, Kelly also needed me. At fifteen wading through this grief was monumental for her. When I did have time with Kelly, it was all I could do to keep my eyes open. I was physically and emotionally exhausted and in a constant state of worry. I had a tough time listening, focusing on anything. I just felt crippled with guilt every time I looked into Kelly's eyes that were pleading with me to take her pain away. Isaiah 66:13 shares, "As a mother comforts her child, so will I comfort you." To those who are in similar situations, I want you to know that God strengthened and guided my path so that I could focus on the child who needed me most. In the parable of The Lost Sheep, Jesus taught his disciples that a good shepherd leaves the ninety-nine to save the one. Megan was my lost sheep and I wanted to save her.

It became my family's new normal for me to stay over with Megan on most nights. I would then come home to be with Kelly one night a week and my husband, Boz, would stay with Megan. It was on one of these nights when I needed to be home with Kelly that I was having a hard time leaving. Although Megan was now resting peacefully, she had been sick all day with a stomach bug. This was extremely dangerous for someone in Megan's condition because of the risk of aspiration and it had been a really difficult day. As Boz and I began the transition for me to go, he calmly walked me to the door and promised all would be fine. Despite his reassuring words, I cried all the way to my car. And . . . speaking of that damn car, it was another source of my misery. It was in desperate need of repair. The car had trouble starting, the heater went on and off, and the radio barely played above a crackle. The silence inside the car was my worst enemy and my head would quickly fill up with my own emotional static.

When I got in the car. I just screamed and screamed out to God: "PLEASE HELP ME! I GIVE UP! I CAN'T TAKE IT ANYMORE." I then just laid my head down on the wheel and closed my eyes for a few minutes. My breath started to calm, and I wiped away my tears, and started the car. Well, the radio was on, without any static and playing the song, "I Will Lift My Eyes" which speaks to the verse from Psalm 121:1-2. I felt a warm and calming embrace cross through me. In that moment, God was present and calmed the rough waters around me giving me the strength to push forward. Just as shared in Psalm 107:29, "He stilled the storm to a whisper; the waves of the sea were hushed."

On another particularly hard night at rehab, I had sent the message out that we were worn and needed to be alone. I sat in our dimly lit room while Megan was resting when I heard a quiet knock on our door. Now if I am being honest, I was having a pity party and was a little mad that the message for no company was not being honored. I opened the door and two individuals from Calvary Church stood with guitars in hand. I said that we were not up for company. They asked if they could play us just one song and I reluctantly agreed. As the gentlemen started to play, tears sprung to my eyes, because they were singing the verse from Psalm 121:1 "I will lift my eyes to the mountain." We then proceeded to talk about the goodness of God's love for hours as Megan peacefully slept. Funny that my pity party disappeared, and the joy of the Lord filled my heart. It would be many days before the sadness would overtake me again.

Eleven months after Megan's accident, as bittersweet as it was, we were all home. Before all this had happened my husband and I had agreed to move our bedroom to the basement to allow for Megan to have her own room for her senior year. My heart broke that Megan never got to sleep in that room because her accident happened before it was finished. Instead, this room became a storage for all the things that we had gathered over the months from being in ICU and our time in rehab. Every time I walked by that room, it was like a stab to my gut, reminding me that it was never going to be filled with the joy of a high school senior getting ready to go off to college. I decided I needed to tackle that room, or it would continue to haunt me. As I was cleaning out Megan's dresser, I found an index card in her writing with the verse Psalm 121:1-2 written out. My heart soared! Megan has read this Psalm and knew where her help came from. Praise God for preparing her with his truth. This verse has been a living life-preserver and always comes to me in verse or song when I feel like I am drowning. Although I continue to make imperfect progress towards this, I know that when I keep my eyes fixed on the Lord my circumstances change for the better, my burdens feel lighter, and I find divine rest in his heavenly peace.

> "But those who hope in the Lord will renew their strength. They will soar on wings like eagles; they will run and not grow weary; they will walk and not be faint."
>
> (Isaiah 40:31)

Meditate on God's Truth and Words:

- Capture the message you think God wants you to hear from this chapter.
- Meditation Verse: Read and meditate on the following verse and reflect on how this applies to your everyday life. Pick out one word that stands out most to you when you read the following verse.
    - "You will call upon Me and come and pray to Me, and I will listen to you. You will seek Me and find Me when you seek me with all your heart." Jeremiah 29:12-13
- Praise Song: Search for the following worship song and listen to it. When you're done, reflect on what you heard and how it made you feel.
    - "I Will Lift My Eyes" by Bebo Norman
- Reflect on the following questions:
    - In what ways do you keep your eyes fixed on the Lord to guide your path?
    - How have you seen God show up in the midst of your storm(s)?
    - Think of situations where you may have felt forsaken. How did you find peace? In what ways did the Lord show up to give you peace?

An Athlete's Heart

> ". . . And let us run with perseverance the race marked out for us, fixing our eyes on Jesus, the pioneer and perfecter of faith . . ."
>
> (Hebrews 12:1b-2a)

Megan was born with a willful spirit and boundless energy. We worked to channel that energy in a variety of ways, including sports, dance, and what ended up being her favorite, cheerleading. Beyond the fun of rooting for the home team, the squad spent much of their time preparing for various competitions. The discipline and rigor that went into preparing for the events was intense, and the girls were in great physical shape. One of my fondest memories of Megan's time as a cheerleader was when they won a national competition hosted at Walt Disney World. When I close my eyes and think of that moment, I can still see the image of Megan jumping for joy and the excitement radiating from her face. God has a way of replaying these precious moments in such detail, that when they appear, they seem divinely placed.

Megan's Cheerleading Team

Megan experienced her own God kiss before the accident when she received the highly honored Spirit Award from her coach. What was uncanny, and godly, about receiving this award was the timing. The award is normally given out at the end of the season banquet, but for some reason, the coach was driven to honor this award to Megan following her Senior Show-Off competition. If the award had been given out at the end of the season banquet, Megan's accident would have already taken place. To this day the coach cannot explain why she broke her tradition that one and only time. I am so thankful that the Holy Spirit must have been on the move in that coach, helping to guide her decision, and in turn, providing Megan with this amazing gift before the accident would change her course for life.

In reflection, another precious gift from the Lord happened on the morning of the accident. Megan was not always one to be warm and fuzzy in showing her feelings, especially during those teenage years. Our morning routine was such that I would shower first, then get the girls up. On most days Megan would still be in the shower when I left for work. In the morning just prior to her accident, as I was pouring my coffee to go, I heard my inner voice whisper, "Stay and enjoy your coffee at home; it's Friday. Relax, don't rush." I chose to listen and sat down to enjoy a solitary moment. Another whisper came to me to "just get up and get to work," and I listened. Just as I was heading out the door, Megan was now out of the shower and at the top of the stairs asking me why I was still home. I told her that I had hung around to tell her I loved her; she then told me she loved me too. Those were the last spoken words between her and me. God put me in that exact spot for the reason of sharing our love verbally with each other before the world would crash down on us just six hours later. Megan was never to speak again, but even today as I look to the top of my stairs, I can still picture my beautiful Megan standing there telling me she loved me. I am so thankful that I listened to my Lord's sweet whisper to be still on that day. I know there are no chance encounters, or coincidences, and that this is a clear example of God's loving hand guiding and preparing me.

The memory of when I first saw Megan in ICU scarred me for life. As much as I felt paralyzed with fear, that superhuman strength of doing whatever it would take to save her was racing through me. As she lay there sleeping, not a scratch on her, I kept asking myself, "How can this be so serious? How can my sweet child be straddling life and death when she looks so peaceful?" I took her hand and out of the depths of my soul I told her to "fight the good fight." I then thought to myself, "Where did that come from?" It was during my devotion time several weeks later, I found my answer in Scripture that was speaking to me from 2 Timothy 4:7, "I have fought the good fight, I have finished the race, I have kept the faith." This became one of my constant prayers, that I will always keep the faith and that I will fight the good fight and when I finish, I will hear the Lord saying to me, "Well done, my faithful one."

Several days of buzzers, monitors, and doctors and nurses rushing in and out, it was finally explained that one of the medical strategies to keep Megan alive while her brain was so swollen, was to make her heart pump at an accelerated pace. They shared that if they could not reduce the brain pressure her heart would simply give out. The doctor equated the accelerated heart rate to running as fast as you can without stopping for four days. I was in shock; how could anyone withstand this pressure? As I prayed, I heard the Lord say, "She has the heart of an athlete; she can withstand this fight." So, with God's grace combined with Megan's strong and perfectly fit body, she was able to fight through all the pressures being put on her most vital organs.

Several weeks following the accident, I was asked to attend the football/cheerleader banquet to receive a donation in Megan's honor. I completely pulled on the Lord's strength to guide me through that acceptance. As I was thanking the guests for their generous donation, I also found myself reinforcing to these young people and their families to work hard at honoring their bodies and to keep their sights on what is good and what would honor God. I thanked the coaches for their work in keeping these kids strong. Two months later, I found myself speaking to thousands of people at a cheerleading competition explaining what the doctors had to do to keep Megan alive and that because of her having the heart of an athlete, she was living and teaching us what was important. Eight months after that I was invited to our city's Sports Women of the Year Award Ceremony. As I walked up to the podium, I was on the verge of tears and felt like I might not be able to speak. I remember praying so hard for the Lord to guide me as my labored steps began to move me forward. The Lord directed me to speak from the innermost level of my pain. As I finished, slightly embarrassed by vulnerability, I saw that most of the attendees had tears in their eyes as well. In giving up so much of my emotions that day, and many following, the Holy Spirit was able to move through many individuals, benefitting Megan and glorifying God. As I prepared to speak at these events, I was continually reminded of the night of the accident when I was standing alone in that bathroom when the Lord said to me, "Be prepared to speak to many." And with each of those early speaking opportunities, and many since, the Lord used me as his vessel and provided me with the words to share and the listener to hear.

As years progressed many great people have come into our lives. One woman, Stephanie, who is a physical education teacher, asked what we thought about getting Megan out into the racing community, surrounded by fresh air and to experience new things. Stephanie asked a friend of hers, Mike who used an adult jogger with his daughter if he would try it out on Megan. He eagerly agreed and we arranged for a date for him to come to the house. On that day as they fit Megan into the jogger and began to run away with her, I remember being so nervous. I felt like my heart was pumping at a runner's rate while I watched in anticipation of Megan's reaction. When they returned, Megan had the biggest smile I had seen in a while. Mike switched the jogger to be trailed by his bike and proceeded to take Megan up a very steep hill near our house. On their way down, all we could hear was Megan's belly laugh. I was thrilled. One of Megan's favorite things to do when she was little was to ride her bike as fast as she could down that same hill. When I heard that laugh it confirmed to me that she was still with us and knew what was going on.

With Megan clearly on board, Stephanie asked if she could hold a fundraiser to get her a stroller. I said yes with trepidation. Over the years we have asked our community to help support us in keeping Megan at home, and I wasn't sure if asking for money for this "nonessential" item was the right thing to do. I put my trust in God and let her loose to raise the funds. With the security and reach of an online fundraising approach, she raised enough money in twenty-four hours to not only cover the cost of the jogger but to pay for the entrance fees for the 5K races for two years! We were so blessed that people recognized Megan's need for fun just as much as for her "essential" supplies. With the 5K races being fundraisers for others, it also allowed Megan to actively serve and be the hands and feet of the Lord, despite her limited capacity.

Faith is not about us having to move mountains; it is about God giving us the strength to move mountains. The Bible says all we need is faith the size of a mustard seed. The mustard seed is one of the smallest seeds on the planet earth. In Matthew 17:20 the Lord says, "Truly I tell you, if you have faith as small as a mustard seed, you can say to this mountain, 'Move from here to there,' and it will move. Nothing will be impossible for you." Growing our faith requires the same commitment and discipline of a strong athlete. An athlete does not just get out there and play their sport. They have been coached by one who knows more about their sport than they do and are disciplined to train to improve their abilities. To build spiritual fitness, we need to pray that the Lord sends us strong spiritual leaders to coach us, to train us, and lead us to victory. We need a team of believers that will encourage us and share their knowledge of the Lord. Jesus was the greatest teacher and a superb coach to his disciples. Just like an athlete, being spiritually fit is a lifestyle. It requires regular time with the Lord so he may speak into our days. The

Lord wants us to walk by faith, not by sight. By listening for His voice in everything we do, everywhere we go, he can keep us on track, guide our steps, and give divine strength for the journey. The world can be overwhelming on any given day, and we are never alone. We just need to run to the Lord because his arms are wide open.

> "His master replied, 'Well done, good and faithful servant! You have been faithful with a few things; I will put you in charge of many things. Come and share your master's happiness!'"
>
> (Matthew 25:21)

Megan in jogging stroller w/ Pat

Meditate on God's Truth and Words:

- Capture the message you think God wants you to hear from this chapter.
- Meditation Verse: Read and meditate on the following verse and reflect on how this applies to your everyday life. Pick out one word that stands out most to you when you read the following verse.
  - "For physical training is of some value, but godliness has value for all things, holding promise for both the present life and the life to come." (1Timothy 4:8)
- Praise Song: Search for the following worship song and listen to it. When you're done, reflect on what you heard and how it made you feel.
  - "Well Done" by The Afters
- Reflect on the following questions:
  - Thinking in terms of your spiritual fitness, how is it with your soul?
  - How do you feel about your relationship with God?
  - What areas of your faith journey are you struggling with or is lacking?
  - When you next pray, ask the Lord specifically how you can grow in your relationship with him.

Prayers Change Everything

> "Do not be anxious about anything, but in every situation, by prayer and petition, with thanksgiving, present your requests to God. And the peace of God, which transcends all understanding, will guard your hearts and your minds in Christ Jesus."
> (Philippians 4:6-7)

Through my faith journey, my prayer life has matured over time. As a child I remember memorizing and reciting the Lord's Prayer, and it always provided me with a feeling of comfort. It still does. I can see myself standing by my father and feeling a great sense of belonging as we recited this prayer in church. My dad died when I was quite young and with that, I lost my formative spiritual leader. Through my young adult years, I remember always feeling somewhat empty and was in search of that same spiritual connection that my father had demonstrated to me.

I went through a variety of paths, some bringing me in a closer relationship with the Lord and some moving me further away.

Just prior to Megan's accident, I remember my prayers being more like a wish list. I prayed for things like an addition to my house, a new car, and for Megan to not go so far away to college. In hindsight, I can now say, "Be careful what you wish for . . . you may just get it." Through God's amazing grace these prayers were all answered - maybe not in the way I originally wanted - but when the need was greatest. A year following Megan's accident, our community built a totally accessible bedroom for her to stay at home, so we got that new addition. A group of dedicated people organized a golf tournament raising enough money to buy our family a new van with a lift to transport Megan, so we got the new car. With the severity of Megan's injuries, she would not go to that out-of-state college, or any college at all. What was important and merciful was the Lord provided for our needs in a way that allowed us to care for Megan at home. No matter our circumstances, and the difficulties we face, prayers have the power to change everything.

Faith is a continual journey to better understand ourselves and deepen the relationship we have with God. Through my storms, I have directly witnessed the transformative power of prayer and the ability to amplify our needs through others praying for us. Back when Megan first had her accident, the internet was new. I was amazed when I discovered a man had put out a prayer request through the web. Later, when I had a chance to meet this man of faith, he brought me boxes filled with the responses from his virtual prayer request. The notes were filled with heartwarming and inspiring words that brought so much love into my home from places near and far. I still have those prayers in a file cabinet in Megan's closet. They consume two whole drawers.

Megan fought hard during her critical time in ICU, and after six weeks in the hospital, she was moved on Christmas Eve to St. Mary's Brain Rehabilitation. We spent eight months there adjusting and accepting the knowledge of the severity of Megan's injuries. It was a difficult time. I witnessed many patients coming into the facility in a similar state as Megan, but then were able to leave walking, talking, or having some level of independence. I prayed and prayed again to the Lord to help me understand why other patients were improving and not my Megan.

As I began to build relationships with other families, their stories began to unfold. The Holy Spirit helped move me from a place of sorrow to a place of hope. My heart now sang for the woman whose daughter was able to heal from her injuries, because she had a two-year-old at home that needed her. I felt joy for the young man who was in a motorcycle accident and had recovered, since his mother was already caring for his brother, who had disabilities of his own. Through my reflective time in prayer, the Lord changed my perspective on the happenings in our lives and those around us. I moved from that feeling of hopelessness and sadness for Megan to wholeheartedly cheering for anyone who made it out of rehab with more independence than when they entered. Life can be heavy, and we are not called to do it through our own strength, but through God's spirit being strong in us. As shared in Romans 12:12, "Be joyful in hope, patient in affliction, faithful in prayer."

As I sit here and write amidst the COVID-19 pandemic that is bringing the whole world to its knees, I am at God's total mercy. My entire family is quarantined in our house, and we are all categorized as being "most vulnerable." Megan because of her compromised state, me because of my autoimmune issues, and for my husband who just received news that the recurrence of lung cancer has also spread to his lymph nodes. In this moment, my mind is reeling with the "what-if's" and fear is once again trying to take over. My mind is unfocused, my head is filled with statistics that I do not want to know about. I am flat-out panicked. So, I sit at this computer, put my head down with tears in my eyes and say to the Lord, "Take this cup from me. I'm worn out; my husband is scared. We are fearful to even leave the house and have been isolated for too long. Oh LORD, please take this cup from me!" As I cry out, I feel a gentleness wash over me and a soothing voice whispering softly to me, "My daughter, I've got this. It is another trial that will eventually glorify me and provide you witness to my never-ending love." I am again reminded of the promise from the Lord to trust in him for he has a plan for each of us and it is for goodness. I let the feeling of peace and hope spread through my entire being. Do I understand it? NO! But I know the Lord, and through all the past experiences, he has shown his heavenly goodness through every storm.

Prayers change everything, even when they are messy, unintelligible, simple, or elegant. When we call out to our Savior, he provides us with the grace and mercy to handle all. I have learned that fear and faith are not compatible. Praying is the number one way for me to directly communicate my fear and needs to the Lord. I found prayers take me to a place where I can face the difficulties, disappointments, and feelings of hopelessness that creep into my days. I pray continually to be released from all the worries of tomorrow, or the regrets of yesterday. I know that when I cry out in pain or anguish, the Lord calms the waters. I've learned to be vulnerable and share my burdens with others and ask directly for their prayers. And through this transparency, I've provided space for others to share their need for prayer back to me. I am now better at disciplining my prayers to be a song of gratitude and praise for the way God is working in my life. I've learned to listen for God's whisper in everything I do and his gentle nudge everywhere I go. He is the one who will keep me on track, guide my steps, and give me strength and peace for the journey.

> 9 "So I say to you: Ask and it will be given to you; seek and you will find; knock and the door will be opened to you. 10 For everyone who asks receives; the one who seeks finds; and to the one who knocks, the door will be opened."
>
> (Luke 11:9-10)

Meditate on God's Truth and Words:

- Capture the message you think God wants you to hear from this chapter.
- Meditation Verse: Read and meditate on the following verse and reflect on how this applies to your everyday life. Pick out one word that stands out most to you when you read the following verse.
    - "But when you ask, you must believe and not doubt, because the one who doubts is like a wave of the sea, blown and tossed by the wind." (James 1:6)
- Praise Song: Search for the following worship song and listen to it. When you're done, reflect on what you heard and how it made you feel.
    - "When We Pray" by Tauren Wells
- Reflect on the following questions:
    - What are some of the ways you have prayed when you have felt closest to the Lord?
    - How can you be more intentional with your prayers?
    - How have you seen the power of prayer work in your life or the lives of others?

Pennies From Heaven

> "In God, whose word I praise—in God I trust and am not afraid. What can mere mortals do to me?"
> (Psalm 56:4)

Pennies are a particular thing, and the value is in the eye of the beholder. They turn up sometimes in the oddest places. We often walk right by them, and other times we may bend down to pick them up. As a young child, I remember my mother saying in her singsong voice, "See a penny, pick it up, and if it is heads up, it's good luck." Well pennies became a great symbol of hope for me during the time Megan was in ICU, and in the years following, they became my pennies from heaven.

The very first time I felt brave enough to leave the ICU, I went with my family to the cafeteria. On our way I spotted a penny. I leaned down to pick it up, and I remember saying to my family, "Heads up, good luck."

As I picked up the penny, I thought about it being a sign of hope and felt a strong rush of peace. We were desperate for signs that Megan was going to live and get better. Oddly, or not so oddly, we all began finding these heads-up pennies all over the hospital. There was even a penny in the elevator doorjamb on the floor of the ICU. It seemed every time I was hyped with worry, or wiped out, a heads-up penny would turn up. I later discovered that some of the girls that Megan helped coach for cheerleading were collecting pennies for our family, and in time, ended up raising hundreds of dollars. Later, Megan's former psychology teacher had started a penny fund in her honor to teach altruism to his classes. So, these little pennies, worth practically nothing, ended up having great value in providing for Megan's needs and my hope.

A year after Megan's accident, I was relaying the story of the pennies that we found in the hospital and the awesome feeling of hope. My friend then shared a story she read about a man who found a penny every day of his life, and he knew it was the Lord speaking to him because the penny reads, "In God we trust." It was like a revelation, a sweet knock over my head. It was now so clear to me that through these pennies, the Lord was sending a message to put our trust in him. I knew immediately that God wanted me to share this testimony of his holy presence with others. As I began to pray on it, I thought of the upcoming golf tournament to raise much needed funds. I bowed my head and said, "Lord, there is a message here that I believe you want people to know. Help me to design a thank you gift using found pennies and I will trust that I will find the appropriate amount." In four months, I personally found the exact number of pennies we needed. I then needed a verse to also put on the bookmark. I asked the Lord to guide me, and he led me to the following verse from Proverbs 3:5-6: "Trust in the Lord with all your heart and lean not on your own understanding; In all your ways submit to him, and he will make your paths straight." With the pennies in hand and the verse to guide, I just needed an image for the background. After searching through hundreds of images, my prayers led me to a beautiful picture of a path in the woods. With the components of the bookmark selected, we were able to produce this handcrafted and godly designed gift to thank the guest for their participation.

Following golf, we all gathered for the awards dinner. The bookmarks had been placed at each place setting. I was asked to speak and knew this would be a wonderful opportunity to share the story behind the creation of the bookmarks. I was able to talk about the power of the Holy Spirit sending us those pennies from heaven, which in turn provided us with many moments of hope and peace. I shared with the group that it was no coincidence that I was able to find the exact number of pennies we needed. I then closed out the dinner in prayer thanking the Lord for the people in the room that were instruments for his provisions.

I noticed a woman waiting patiently to talk to me and when it was her turn, she approached me with tears in her eyes and breathlessly asked me where I found the image that was on the bookmark. I shared that after sorting through hundreds of pictures and much prayer, I felt led to the one I chose. The woman shared that her sister had been in a horrible car accident and suffered injuries much like Megan. One of the few things that her sister responded to following her accident was a poster that hung in her room with this same image that was on the bookmark. In fact, this woman had commissioned someone to paint a mural of this same image in her sister's room because she had such a response to it. We hugged, we cried, and I shared the love of the Lord as we prayed together. The woman then trembling, asked the Lord for forgiveness in turning her back on his love and for all the anger she had displayed since her sister's accident. As the woman emptied her soul to the Lord, she looked once again at the bookmark and noticed the date of the penny on her bookmark, that had been randomly placed at her place setting, was her sister's birth year. The chills permeated through both of us. This was no coincidence but another example of the Holy Spirit on the move.

In Hebrews 1:11, faith is described as having confidence in what we hope for and assurance about what we do not see. Relying on hope and faith is like learning to see in the dark. Hope is not a wish list, or something we receive through positive thinking. Hope is a supernatural gift that represents the Lord's Spirit moving through each of us. Jesus explains the Holy Spirit as his gift of peace and hope for us all. When we put our trust in the Lord, we harvest abundant peace and hope in our daily lives. There are signs everywhere of this presence, and just like pennies from heaven, we need to be open to the messages that surround us. Hope is an essential part of life as a believer and when we let circumstances control our hope, we end up with a conditional hope that is not grounded in faith but in our own understanding. When we rely on our faith, we have access to a more powerful hope that changes us. As we go through each day, we need to be open to the voice or the nudge from the Holy Spirit. We may find that we are not just a receiver of God's provision but the deliverer of one. With the Holy Spirit working through each of us, the hands of the Almighty may just be at the end of our own arms.

Bookmark

> "I will say of the Lord, 'He is my refuge and my fortress, my God, in whom I trust.'"
>
> (Psalm 91:2)

Meditate on God's Truth and Words:

- Capture the message you think God wants you to hear from this chapter.
- Meditation Verse: Read and meditate on the following verse and reflect on how this applies to your everyday life. Pick out one word that stands out most to you when you read the following verse.
    - "You will keep in perfect peace those whose minds are steadfast because they trust in you." (Isaiah 26:3)
- Praise Song: Search for the following worship song and listen to it. When you're done, reflect on what you heard and how it made you feel.
    - "Trust in You" by Laura Daigle
- Reflect on the following questions:
    - How do you step out in faith when all is not well?
    - Have you been comforted by the Holy Spirit when you put your full trust in the Lord?
    - God is good all the time. Where have you seen the good come out of the bad?

Let My House Be Joyful

> "You turned my wailing into dancing; you removed my sackcloth and clothed me with joy, that my heart may sing your praises and not be silent. Lord my God, I will praise you forever."
>
> (Psalm 30:11-12)

Megan was still in rehab, and we were preparing to bring her home. A nurse on the floor asked another family if I could come and see their lift system. I was graciously welcomed, and upon my visit we sat at the kitchen table for a few minutes getting to know one another. I know our hearts went out to each other knowing each other's pain. We eventually got around to seeing the lift and it was impressive. As we went back to the table to talk some more, their daughter's nurse was introduced to me. She sat on a stool around the corner. The family went on to show me their house rules and how they managed their daughter's care. They had many negative things to share about working with the agencies, nurses and the complexity that goes with caring for a brain-injured daughter. It all became overwhelming, and I quickly excused myself. As soon as I got into my car, the tears began to fall. I was feeling so down, and once again the hopelessness was beginning to set in. As I was sobbing, I lifted my eyes and began to call out to the Lord to help us create a joyful home, where all were welcomed and happy. Decades later He continues to keep that promise, and our home is known to welcome all with a spirit of joy and love.

I remember the first day with our part-time nurse. I hadn't had a chance to meet her yet before I had to leave for work. I left my mother in charge and when I walked in hours later, there sat the same nurse that I had met months earlier at the home of the family that showed us the lift. Dee was her name, and we recognized each other immediately. Dee shared with me that she had seen the different news articles concerning Megan and she prayed, "Dear Lord, please, let me share in the joy that family has. Let me be a part of the miracle." He answered her prayers with a position with us. We loved Dee, and she became part of our family. She stayed for thirteen years, which is rare for a part-time nurse. Our full-time nurse Chris stayed with us for seventeen years. She too was family. We now have a long list of caregivers helping us to care for Megan, which is unheard of in the private nursing world. They each bring their own kind of joy, and we love everyone who God brings to our door. I know it is God's answer to my tear-filled prayer to make my house a joyful place that honors his glory.

When we brought Megan home, the Lord sent us wonderful friends who would volunteer and help me bathe Megan and put her to bed each night. I lovingly call these women our "bath girls." I am still in awe of their loyalty and commitment. Our longest standing "bath girl" was Debbie coming every Sunday night for years. In close second was Stephanie who usually came to us on Saturday nights. She introduced us to many other angels willing to help. My longtime childhood friends Lori and Kathe would try to come on Friday nights, and it always renewed me. We used this time of fellowship to carry each other's burdens and sing praise for the blessings that were bestowed. We laughed, we cried, we solved each other's problems; sharing each other's joys and heartaches.

One night it was snowing heavily, and Kathe and Lori were unable to make it. I was at a low point and had really been looking forward to their company. I went on with the bath routine. Megan was now in bed, and I was rubbing lotion on her feet. The tears began to fall, and I started talking to the Lord. It was sort of a prayer but more of just a conversation with Jesus about how he washed his disciples' feet and shared stories of how God wants us to serve one another. The tears and sadness would not abate, but my spiritual connection with the Lord lifted my heart.

I left Megan to rest and braved the snow to go outside and get the mail. As I walked down the driveway, my tears continued to fall. I just couldn't shake the heaviness I had been feeling. I opened the mailbox and found a package. I was curious to see what it was and hurried back inside. As I opened the package, I found a note from a young man I had never met. The letter went on to explain that the summer before, this man had edited a news broadcast about Megan's story. He had since moved from Rochester to California and was now working for a famous musician, Jim Brickman. This young man remembered that Megan responded to music and had the chance to share her story with this artist. Mr Brickman then encouraged him to send some of his CDs to Megan for her healing. The music was joyous! It immediately took my sadness away for the night. I thanked God for his sweet kiss of reminding me that his holy presence is always with us. Just like what is shared in Zephaniah 3:17, "The Lord your God is with you, the Mighty Warrior who saves. He will take great delight in you; in his love he will no longer rebuke you but will rejoice over you with singing."

The Lord has brought that spirit of hope and joy into our house, helping us attract good people to support us with Megan's needs. Each moment the Holy Spirit is moving in us, through us, and deeply desires to connect with us in every way possible. God uses each of us, and all our trials to promote his love and in doing so, he is able to lift both the giver and receiver.

Just recently in our twenty-third year of caring for Megan after her accident, we were in the doctor's office for Megan's physical. My doctor, who cares for our entire family, looked at me and said that I did not look well. I was plain broken, worn out, depressed, and any sense of joy was hard to find. In addition, Megan's health status was bearing truth to some of the negative things that happen with the duration of being in her condition. I started to cry, and our wonderful doctor said, "This too will pass." She comforted me by saying Megan has been cared for in a wonderful way, and that our house and family were known and admired for our joyful spirit. After the appointment, I was thinking she was right, and I praised God for his blessing in answering my prayer of making our home welcoming, peaceful, and loving. I know the Lord wants us to cast all our cares on him for he wants us to be joyful. Just like what is shared in Proverbs 17:22, "A cheerful heart is good medicine, but a crushed spirit dries up the bones."

No matter our circumstances, each one of us has the power to reclaim our joy. This positive spirit, even in the direst of situations, is a true window to our soul. Each day our ability to restore and renew ourselves exists when we are a believer. The Lord invites us to put our fears under his feet and allow him to crush them. I know personally that when I am focused on my relationship with the Lord, my fears are mitigated. When I take my eyes off him, my mind quickly brims over with my worry and fear. But a believer has the power to center their well-being, by being open to God's divine presence of hope delivered through the

Holy Spirit. I am often reminded of this when I read this verse from Matthew 14:29-32, "Then Peter got down out of the boat, walked on the water and came toward Jesus. But when he saw the wind, he was afraid and, beginning to sink, cried out, 'Lord, save me!' Immediately Jesus reached out his hand and caught him. 'You of little faith,' he said, 'why did you doubt?' And when they climbed into the boat, the wind died down."

When we feel joy, it is God dwelling in us, and it's important that we start and end our days with what we are grateful for. For it is not joy that makes us grateful, it is being grateful that makes us joyful. As much as I wish I did not have to carry these burdens, I am also experiencing the amazing blessings that go with walking through these life storms with Jesus. No one knows how difficult and painful life can be, better than the Lord. I now see more clearly that peace and joy are not the absence of trouble; it is the presence of God. Each day is a precious gift from God, and we can choose to live in a way that either adds to God's glory or distracts from it. We can choose to live in an attitude of resentment, anger, fear; or we can choose to pursue the joy of Christ. Joy is a gift to you from God and it comes from within because that is where the joy of the Lord lives.

> "Do not grieve, for the joy of the Lord is your strength."
>
> (Nehemiah 8:10b)

Meditate on God's Truth and Words:

- Capture the message you think God wants you to hear from this chapter.
- Meditation Verse: Read and meditate on the following verse and reflect on how this applies to your everyday life. Pick out one word that stands out most to you when you read the following verse.
    - "You have made known to me the paths of life; you will fill me with joy in your presence." (Acts 2:28)
- Praise Song: Search for the following worship song and listen to it. When you're done, reflect on what you heard and how it made you feel.
    - "Alive & Breathing" by Matt Maher
- Reflect on the following questions:
    - What is the difference between happiness and joy?
    - What are you most grateful for? How can your gratitude for these things bring you joy?

God Guides My Career Path

5 "If any of you lacks wisdom, you should ask God, who gives generously to all without finding fault, and it will be given to you.6 But when you ask, you must believe and not doubt, because the one who doubts is like a wave of the sea, blown and tossed by the wind."

(James 1:5-6)

When the girls were little, my husband worked in a variety of roles in the restaurant business, and when I could, I'd also pick up shifts to bring in extra income. Money was a bit tight, but somehow, we always made it work. Looking back, I feel blessed to have had that time to be with the girls during most of their waking hours. Once they were both settled into school, I decided it was time for me to pursue that degree I always wanted. I had credits toward my bachelor's degree in psychology and was always drawn to the idea of becoming a teacher. With much planning, support from my family, and a few loans from the bank, I was able to get myself back to school. It took some time, and after several years, and a lot of demanding work, I received my master's degree in special education.

One of my first full-time teaching assignments was in the city school district in an under-served area. I was asked to lead a class of emotionally challenged young boys for what was supposed to be a temporary assignment. The principal handed me their files, each extremely thick with detail and incident reports. After pouring through the files, I realized this was not a job for the faint of heart. The previous teacher had even resigned after being beaten down— emotionally and physically—while teaching this class.

I showed up on my first day as their temporary teacher, and as I anticipated, the boys pulled out all the stops on me. It was a very rough day, but at the end of class, I shared with them that I was heading straight to the district office to beg for this job. The boys looked at me like I had three heads. I went on to say how much I wanted to be their teacher and that I was going to fight hard for the permanent role. What the boys didn't know was that the principal had offered the job to me if I wanted it. The next day, I showed up with a cake and balloons and shared excitedly that I had two things that I wanted to celebrate with them. The first was my birthday and the second thing was that my good fight had worked. I went on to share that the district made me their permanent teacher. I looked at each of them with deep care and told them that no matter what, no matter how badly they acted up, I would always love every one of them. Because every teacher knows they have a special place in their heart for their first class.

Through my time at this school, I saw many heartaches, but nothing prepared me for the day a young girl was stabbed to death on the front steps of our school just as everyone was arriving for the day. The image of that beautiful child dying in front of my eyes was so crucifying it created a scar for life. Although the darkness of that day was blinding to us all, the strength of the Lord shined so deeply through the victim's family, it was incredible to witness. Day after day they came to the school and provided such comfort to us as we walked through this horrific tragedy. In the many years that followed that tragic incident, I continually reflect on that family. I continue to be awestruck on the strength and love they shared with us. Where did this strength come from? How could someone lose a child in such a tragic way yet be filled with more love than hate? That was a question I asked myself for a long time, until I was then faced with my own loss. I soon realized for myself that the only way to truly keep on living through life-altering storms is to stay in active relationship with God. The Lord uses these circumstances to transform, refine and purify our hearts.

With that in mind, it was the first summer following Megan's accident, and it was a beautiful time to be home and on break from my teaching job. I was starting to feel like things were falling into place with keeping Megan at home, all except for my job. The staff at school and my coworkers had felt so sorry for me and were letting me deliver less than my best. This was personally unacceptable to me. One Monday I had a phone conference with my vice principal about the position for the coming school year. She was insisting on a classroom that I knew I was not going to be successful in. We went back and forth every day for a week. It finally dawned on me on that Friday morning, with all the chaos in my head, I had not spent the time in intentional prayer asking the Lord to guide my direction. When the call came from the vice principal to talk again, I stated that I needed to pray about it. I am not sure if my vice principal was a believer and could understand my need to be in prayer or was rolling her eyes on the other end of the line. Regardless I spoke boldly through my faith and told her that I would get back to her with an answer on Monday.

After the call, I spent hours in prayer with the Lord. I started by asking for forgiveness for trying to control this decision on my own. In that moment, I surrendered my next steps over to God. I prayed very intentionally about what I needed. I asked God for a job that would renew my energy, in a role that would give me purpose—and maybe even help me accept Megan's accident. As I talked through my list of needs, I finished with the need for flexibility so that I could leave Megan every morning and feel that it was okay. In Isaiah 30:21 it says, "Whether you turn to the right or to the left, your ears will hear a voice behind you, saying, 'This is the way; walk in it.'"

The next morning, I went to the mailbox and there was a letter from the city school district that had been sent to all the special education teachers in the region. The letter was to notify us about an available position for a newly created role. It was for a special education teacher to work with a cross-specialist team to evaluate the need for assistive technologies for children of different abilities. The role of the special education teacher would consult with teachers, parents, and medical staff for children with traumatic brain injury. Wow! I had just spent a year working with each of these professions during Megan's rehabilitation. I had been studying the brain and the effects of trauma since her accident. In a state of disbelief, I sat down to reread everything. When I picked up the envelope, I noticed the date stamp, and it was really no surprise to me that the date mailed was the day before: the day I had surrendered my decision to God.

This job checked all the boxes of what I had cried out for. The best part was that the position was part-time with full-time benefits and gave me the flexibility I prayed for. Over the next several weeks I went through the process of applying and interviewing for the role. When I was called in for my final interview, I knew the job was going to be mine before they even offered it to me—which they did. This role was a divine gift to me from God and is a perfect example of the Lord guiding my path and preparing me for his future will. In Psalm 32:8 it says, "I will instruct you and teach you in the way you should go; I will counsel you with my loving eye on you." God is always in the driver's seat, and my career path was well navigated by him. I know that the Lord puts people in our path or puts us in the path of others to confirm and advance his will.

I remember when I met with my first family. I looked them straight in the eye, with my heart filled with overflowing compassion and empathy, and I told them that I would treat their child as my own. They could trust me to always fight for the best interest of their child. These were God's words speaking through me, to them. I could see the burdens they were shouldering beginning to lift. I ended up spending twelve years in this role, which eventually became a full-time position, and worked with hundreds of students and their families. The knowledge I gained, and the relationships I forged during this journey were priceless. I even had the chance to earn a national certification to be a Brain-Based Teaching Specialist. I probably would have finished my career on the team, but I began battling a variety of autoimmune issues and was finding it increasingly difficult to trek to and from the many schools each day. Near the end of my time in that role, I received the diagnosis that I had multiple sclerosis (MS). As is shared in Ecclesiastes 3:1, "There is a time for everything, and a season for every activity under the heavens." And with that, I trusted God to lead me down his path in new ways.

When I was a student teacher while working on my master's degree, I was advised by one of my colleagues to avoid roles that I would get too emotionally involved in. Upon graduation, when I was asked what I wanted to do, I usually would respond with what I didn't think I wanted which included working with kindergarten age, or children with multiple disabilities. I once again found myself on my knees praying for a position that I could use my experiences that would help me tolerate the conditions associated with my MS. With God putting light to my path, I was informed of a job opening by a colleague, who thought the position would be perfect for me. Ironically this new role would be for a kindergarten teacher working with children with multiple disabilities. When walking with God, hindsight always seems to be 20/20. It was so clear to me how God had been preparing me for this position for years. These children were some of the most underserved in our district, with many of them living in very vulnerable situations outside the school hours. I poured everything I had into it—I was freed up to teach and be present as God's servant. I was even allowed to pray with the children, their parents, and other coworkers. I was able to get others to view these children through the lens of the Lord. Through the work with these angels on earth, many lives were transformed inside and outside the classroom.

Unfortunately, my health continued to be on a downward slide and after ten years serving these children and their families, I ended up having to retire much earlier than I had planned. Following that role, God blessed me with the most joyous job of all. I get to teach the wonders of the world to my beautiful granddaughter, who came to us in her own miraculous way, brightening our lives beyond measure. Jeremiah 29:11 indicates that God has a definite plan to prosper us and give us hope. We will all go through seasons in our lives. Seasons that are filled with incredible joy and good fortune, and seasons that may be filled with pain and despair. Through these crooked paths we often have more questions than answers. God wants us to be in a two-way dialogue with him to wrestle through these questions so he can provide greater clarity on his plans and purposes. We live in a broken world, but God promises us that if we follow him, we will have eternal peace. We just need to seek God with all our heart, in all things. God delights in taking ordinary people, like you and me, and providing us with the power to do extraordinary things.

> "Although the Lord gives you the bread of adversity and the water of affliction, your teachers will be hidden no more; with your own eyes you will see them. Whether you turn to the right or to the left, your ears will hear a voice behind you, saying, 'This is the way; walk in it.'"
>
> (Isaiah 30:20-21)

Student from class

Meditate on God's Truth and Words:

- Capture the message you think God wants you to hear from this chapter.
- Meditation Verse: Read and meditate on the following verse and reflect on how this applies to your everyday life. Pick out one word that stands out most to you when you read the following verse.
    - "Show me your ways, Lord, teach me your paths. Guide me in your truth and teach me, for you are God my Savior, and my hope is in you all day long." (Psalm 25:4-5)
- Praise Song: Search for the following worship song and listen to it. When you're done, reflect on what you heard and how it made you feel.
    - "They Will" by Hillary Scott
- Reflect on the following questions:
    - Looking back, hindsight being 20/20, where has your path aligned to God's will?
    - When has God guided your path? Was it easy to follow?
    - How do you stay close and be still with God so he can guide your path?

Megan's Bed and My Sleep

"Come to me, all you who are weary and burdened, and I will give you rest. Take my yoke upon you and learn from me, for I am gentle and humble in heart, and you will find rest for your souls."

(Matthew 11:28-29)

Megan had been cared for at home for over twelve years and was about to turn thirty. It was sometimes hard to think of her as an adult, because her needs were like caring for an infant. As this milestone birthday fell upon us, I knew it was time to shift from thinking of her as a child to honoring her as an adult. I went to work on clearing out the cheerleader memorabilia and began to transform her room. One item in her room that I absolutely hated, for many reasons, was her hospital bed. This bed had limited features and the sterile look that reminded me of her being in the hospital. From the time we brought her home to us, we were warned that the two primary dangers to her well-being would be bed sores that could lead to dangerous infections and pneumonia that would be her demise. Megan isn't paralyzed and she can feel pain; a bed sore would be extremely painful to endure. We were diligent about manually rotating Megan's body from side to side to help reduce any fluids in her lungs and to avoid the onset of a bed sore. This included me waking up every three hours each night to complete the rotations. With the redesign of her room being a spark for change, I began to research available options for a new bed but was having a tough time finding what I was looking for. So, I did what I had come to rely on in these situations—pray intentionally and trust in the Lord to provide.

It was around this time when I was working for an assistive technology and medical management team. One of my responsibilities was to attend an annual education conference and this year it was in Florida. Even though traveling to Florida in January from Rochester, NY, sounded like a nice opportunity, it was not something I was looking forward to. I do not do well in crowds, and this conference was one of the most highly attended of its kind. I knew the exhibit space would be massive and would be buzzing with conference attendees. Once there, I took advantage of getting an early start to the exhibit hall to beat the rush of people, and I was lucky—all was relatively quiet. I began speaking to a vendor about "eye gaze" computer technology. I thought about how the children at our schools might benefit, and how this technology might work for Megan.

I was deep in thought and neglected to notice that the ballroom had filled up with conference attendees. I was positioned in the back of the ballroom and didn't see any way to escape. I started to feel the signs of a panic attack coming on. I took several deep breaths and went to an empty corner and started to pray. As I did, that wisp of calm enveloped me. I started to stand up when I saw in my direct line-of-sight an exhibitor's booth that was showcasing a beautiful piece of furniture that was a hospital bed. I kind of shook my head since this type of product was out-of-place amongst the other exhibit booths. This was one of those unexplainable coincidences that was most certainly a God kiss. With a determined pace, I quickly made my way to the salesperson and began firing questions at him. It was exactly what I had been searching for, and more. The vendor spent over twenty minutes sharing with me all the notable features, which included the automation needed to rotate Megan's body. The salesperson had me lay down on the bed and I remember the feeling of just floating, and the verse from Psalm 23:2-3 came to mind, "He makes me lie down in green pastures, he leads me beside quiet waters, he refreshes my soul. He guides me along the right paths for his name's sake." I then asked the vendor why he was even at this type of conference versus a medical supply conference. He shared that he was just in the beginning stages of expanding his business out of British Columbia and had signed up for the conference in error. I smiled to myself knowing that this was a testament that the Holy Spirit was on the move. I finally got around to asking the price for this bed and he said $25,000. I choked a bit, put on my poker face, asked for a brochure, and excused myself. I continued with the afternoon sessions, but I could not stop thinking about all that transpired that morning. Later that evening I was sharing with my colleagues what had happened and how strongly I felt the presence of God. I knew that the women were not all believers, but I wanted to share my belief that the Lord was sending me a sign that Megan was going to get this bed.

I returned home and all the usual craziness of life piled on me. I only had a chance to share my experience at the conference with a few of my friends. A brief time had passed and one of my good friends came to me and said she wanted to do something to help raise funds for Megan to get that bed. We were months out from doing our annual golf fundraiser. She was really motivated to do something now. A few days later she called and had come up with a great idea to host a sale for prom dresses. Work began right away. We sought out donations of new or gently used dresses from many different networks and planned to sell the dresses for a price of $25. The Holy Spirit was clearly present and moved through many people to make this event successful. In a month, we were able to secure over four hundred dresses including brand-new dresses from a local bridal shop. My husband's boss donated the use of his largest party room, a jewelry dealer agreed to share 20% of her sales from the event, and even the DJ donated money to us for each booking he made from being at the event. A few days leading up to the event, we held a fashion show that was covered by a local morning news show which generated a great turnout. Overall, we sold well over three hundred dresses making a profit of over $7,500. We then continued to pay this good work forward and donated the remaining dresses to an underserved area allowing seventy-five girls to find the perfect dress for their prom, at no cost to them.

With all the publicity from the prom dress sale, donations for Megan's bed continued to find their way to our mailbox. That August we had our annual golf tournament and raised more money than ever. Despite all these earnest efforts, we were still about $5,000 short of our goal. I continued to take a leap of faith. I asked a friend to begin the search to finally purchase this bed. This was no easy task because there was not a distributor in the state of New York. Our friend then had to go through a process to become an authorized distributor for the company that I had originally met earlier that year at the conference. You can imagine the letdown I felt when we discovered the $25,000 bed was now priced at $35,000, and we were now $10,000 short. I continued to trust in God's timing and forced myself to be patient.

A few months later my dear mother-in-law died unexpectedly and had left each of her granddaughters $10,000. Although her passing was incredibly heartbreaking for all of us, God is always good, and out of every tough situation, there are blessings to be thankful for. Through this devastating loss to our family, the blessing to finally have the money to purchase this bed was provided to us. We immediately put the wheels in motion for this purchase and the timing couldn't be more dire. Megan had a tough summer, and the beginning of a bed sore was taking hold. Her nurses and I worked tirelessly to keep her skin intact, free of infection and to address the pain. It was during this time that we received the call from the medical supply company that they had sourced an available bed for us. It was used but in beautiful shape. The family agreed to sell it for $30,000. We were elated and set a date for delivery.

The day the bed arrived, we were all extremely excited. I could not stop praising God. As the gentleman finished training us on how to use and care for the bed, he commented on our faith. He began to share with us more background on how this bed came about. Apparently when the bed became available, the distributor was on vacation enjoying a large family reunion. His partner had called to tell him about the availability of this bed. The family that was selling the bed shared that they would offer it to the first person that was available to pick it up. The gentleman that was enjoying his family vacation had the only truck that was equipped to transport this bed securely. This same gentleman talked over the situation with his wife. Although the time at the family reunion was important, they both felt strongly there was someone in need of this bed. The only choice then was to go and get it. He then left his family and traveled a day and half to retrieve the bed. Later, when he got to the office, his partner said they just received a call from a medical supply company who knew of a family that had been tirelessly searching for this type of bed. Of course, that family was us. They immediately called back our provider to confirm that this bed met all the requirements. The sale was then finalized that day.

This story is a bit tangled, but God is a master weaver and can fit everything into a pattern for good. Although the timeline to get this bed was longer than we wanted, God worked through many to provide us with what we needed exactly when we needed it most. I am so grateful that the Holy Spirit led many to provide us with the best of beds to ensure Megan's well-being and to give me the ability to finally lie down in the green pastures of rest. Praise be to God!

> "Truly my soul finds rest in God; my salvation comes from him. Truly he is my rock and my salvation; he is my fortress; I will never be shaken."
>
> (Psalm 62:1-2)

Megan and Sophia on her bed

Meditate on God's Truth and Words:

- Capture the message you think God wants you to hear from this chapter.
- Meditation Verse: Read and meditate on the following verse and reflect on how this applies to your everyday life. Pick out one word that stands out most to you when you read the following verse.
  - "This is how we know that we belong to the truth and how we set our hearts at rest in his presence. . ." (1 John 3:19)
- Praise Songs: Search for the following worship song and listen to it. When you're done, reflect on what you heard and how it made you feel.
  - "Be Still" by Kristene DiMarco
- Reflect on the following questions:
  - What does it mean to you to rest your mind versus rest your soul?
  - How could you be more intentional about resting your soul in God?

Surrendering For Peace

> "To shine on those living in darkness and in the shadow of death, to guide our feet into the path of peace."
>
> (Luke 1:79)

As I sit here in reflection, I know that surrendering it all - every worry, fear, and panic to the Lord is the secret sauce to peace, yet I continue to make imperfect progress in doing this. In fact, the more difficult the situation, the more I want to control it. When I hold onto these hardships, the storms just seem to increase with intensity and find myself buried under the force of it all. When I turn it all over to God, my circumstances change. I know when I am connected to the Lord, my resilience is strong. The true peace of God is found under the weight of tough times. When Jesus left us, he gave us the gift of the holy spirit which provides us a solid rock of faith to stand on.

During the critical times of Megan's injury, there were meetings with hospital staff as well as individual doctors. The swelling in Megan's brain was not going down; we did not know hour to hour if she was going to live or not. I often found myself saying to those around me, "Don't ask me to choose between fighting and giving up on Megan." The night before her eighteenth birthday, everything went downhill. Megan had not been stable since she changed rooms. The move had caused her to come close to heart failure and the pressures on her brain were at the highest they had been. Every minute the pressure remained at those levels her brain was being more damaged. The doctor on call told me that I should prepare to decide whether to continue treatment. It was now that dire. As much as I wanted to be in control my whole life, I did not want to be in control of making a decision like this. I was beside myself and stumbled blindly towards the family waiting room prepared to share what was ahead.

When I walked in the room my husband Boz was sound asleep, and my daughter Kelly was sitting there silently sobbing. At that moment, I bowed my head. I surrendered control and was prepared to embrace God's will for what loomed ahead. I sat down calmly next to Kelly and began talking to her in a soothing voice saying that all would be well. When Kelly was asleep, I walked slowly back to the room. As I entered, Megan was basked in a soft light, and the monitor showed that her brain pressure and heart rate were stable. She was sleeping so peacefully. I sat down beside her and picked up my Bible. I found James 5:7, which speaks to believers being patient in all trials and tribulations until the coming of the Lord. The result of this patience is a perfected faith which can't be shaken by doubt or fear.

I've always been impressed with strong believers. Mother Teresa is one of them with her commitment, her mission and her faithful walk with Jesus. I was reminded of the time that the Holy Spirit nudged me and brought me peace through her words. It had been days of grim times and I needed to take a break and just get out of the hospital. I took a walk and stopped at a local bookstore. As I entered the store, I was feeling a little light-headed and stepped down an aisle to catch my breath. I was flat-out spent and as I leaned against the shelf for support a small book fell off and hit my head. Feeling a bit annoyed, I bent down to retrieve it and to my surprise it was a book of spiritual support from Mother Teresa. I knew that the Lord wanted me to read this, and as small as the book was, it provided me a mighty amount of comfort and peace. With the Holy Spirit on the move, there was another amazing connection to Mother Teresa that was revealed to me in the months ahead.

During the time at the hospital, I had noticed a young woman walking with her mother, up and down the halls. On many occasions I asked them to join us in the family lounge. One day they finally agreed, and we began to visit more regularly. I discovered they were both from India, and the young woman shared her story of the storm that changed her life. It was on her honeymoon when she and her husband were in a horrible car crash. Her husband died instantly, and she laid for months in the hospital unresponsive due to massive internal injuries. Medical teams were preparing the family for end-of-life decisions. The woman's brother, located in the States, could not make this decision alone and needed his mother and eldest brother to travel from India. It took several months to get their visa approved. Once they arrived, the mother sat vigilantly behind her daughter's bed and fervently prayed. To everyone's amazement the injured woman began to respond. Although with several years of surgeries and therapies ahead of her, she was going to survive. This initial sharing provided space for a beautiful friendship to emerge. Over the course of weeks, we would walk together, and pray together and sometimes just be still together. One day this young woman shared with me that prior to getting married she lived in Calcutta and worked as a missionary with Mother Teresa. She went on to share that she had been corresponding with Mother Teresa to update her on her progress. In her letters, she had asked Mother Teresa to also pray for Megan. It was powerful for me to know that the Lord was working mightily to generate love around the world for Megan and our family.

Fast forward twenty-three years and I'm sitting here the week after the 2020 presidential election with anxiety in the pit of my stomach. Enough is enough. Everywhere I turn I see tragedy and trauma as the fabric of our nation is literally breaking down right in front of my eyes. The level of violence, hatred, and lack of care for one another on public display is deeply disturbing. With all this going on, COVID continues to rage, and my entire family has been left distraught. It was simply too much to bear and the stress of it all was adding fuel to my despair. I couldn't take it anymore. I just laid my head down on my desk. My fear was in direct battle with my faith - and fear was winning. The heaviness of depression was weighing me down. I could feel the devil getting his hold on me. I knew I couldn't stay in this space; I needed to "FAITH" it. I needed to surrender all my worries and fears to the Lord so he could strengthen me.

As I reflect on what I have learned through following Mother Teresa, I think about the book, "Total Surrender" by Stacey Loper. The book reveals, through Mother Teresa's personal letters, her own struggle with her faith. For decades Mother Teresa wrestled with God's existence, and her own feeling of abandonment from him. Despite her discouragement, Mother Teresa remained steadfast in her vows because she knew it was, she, who was abandoning her trust in God's will. In her words Mother Teresa professed that the only way to face fear in turmoil is to totally surrender it all to the Divine. And when we do this, we will be absolutely free.

> "Now may the Lord of peace himself give you peace at all times and in every way. The Lord be with all of you."
>
> (2 Thessalonians 3:16)

Meditate on God's Truth and Words:

- Capture the message you think God wants you to hear from this chapter.
- Meditation Verse: Read and meditate on the following verse and reflect on how this applies to your everyday life. Pick out one word that stands out most to you when you read the following verse.
    - "Grace, mercy, and peace from God the Father and from Jesus Christ, the Father's Son will be with us in truth and love." (2 John 1:3)
- Praise Song: Search for the following worship song and listen to it. When you're done, reflect on what you heard and how it made you feel.
    - "Peace" by Bethel Music feat. We The Kingdom
- Reflect on the following questions:
    - Is it hard for you to let go, let God? What could you be doing more of, or less of, to surrender to the Lord for that unexplainable peace?
    - What is the difference between giving up and surrendering?
    - Why do you think it is important to surrender to God?
    - Reflect on times when you faced fear with faith and when you faced fear with your own control—what brought you more peace? What would make it easier to let go and let God?

Blind Faith

"For we live by faith, not by sight."
(2 Corinthians 5:7)

I know that the strongest declaration of faith comes during the moments when our lives are seemingly at the worst. We are told to hold onto faith and not circumstances. Despite the number of times that God has provided for my family, I'm still human and walking by faith is not always easy for me. When I'm in a free-fall mode, weighted down by fear, the devil starts stirring up the storms. I then find myself moving farther away from what keeps me close to the Lord. As I choose to turn to the Lord, I am able to dig into my spiritual resilience, and remain steadfast in my faith. I know that the Lord has us covered. Even in the darkest moments, when I'm blinded, I can see the light.

It had been three months since the accident, and we were still in the rehab facility. Megan was not meeting the recovery goals, and the insurance company was in the process of evaluating the need for continued coverage. We were called in for a meeting with the doctor where he shared the recent MRI results that revealed the full extent of Megan's brain injuries. Her brain was now a third smaller because of the additional damage that occurred during the periods of swelling. As the meeting closed, I felt the panic flow from every fiber of my being. What were we to do? Megan was not ready to be discharged, how would we take care of her? We were beside ourselves. Boz headed home and I headed back to Megan's room. I was so distraught, I called one of my sisters in hysterics and within the hour, both my sisters were by my side. It was a night I will not forget. We cried, we laughed, and we talked for a long time about what to do. As they were leaving, with my armor of dangerous confidence, I declared to them both that I had turned everything over to God's hands. There was no controlling this and I had to surrender the next steps to the Lord and trust that Megan's needs would be provided for. I know some people think it is a bit reckless when a believer says they are going to turn it all over to God, but it is a true testament of their belief. Just like what is shared in Hebrews 11:1, "Now faith is confidence in what we hope for and assurance about what we do not see."

A few weeks later another meeting took place that would inform the insurance carrier's decision for extended coverage. The therapists and head nurses gave their reports at the meeting and then were asked to leave. The neurologists stated that Megan did not have any functional use of her body and most likely never would. They also felt that cognitively she did not have any awareness of her surroundings. They basically said in so many words to put Megan into a nursing home and get on with our life. With emotions peppering every word I stated that we were getting on with our lives and that we had accepted Megan's situation. I then went on to say that we were trusting in God to direct our next steps. In that moment, I felt myself move from powerless to powerful. In Isaiah 40:29 it is shared, "He gives strength to the weary and increases the power of the weak." As the meeting continued, I could sense that things were getting a bit heated, and tempers were about to explode. I asked to end the meeting to give us time to process what was shared.

After the meeting, I walked numbly back to Megan's room. I was shocked to find one of the 'toughest' resident neurologists sitting with her. I immediately panicked and asked if she was okay. He explained that although he did not work with Megan, he knew that I never left her alone. He had noticed that the family meeting was running long, and the therapist working with Megan had to go on to her next patient. He decided to take his break in her room and read her the paper. My heart was filled by his kindness. As he left, he said that he had heard it was a difficult meeting, but he told me to never give up on her. I thanked the Lord for putting that man by Megan's bedside. That loving act, at the hands of the Holy Spirit, gave me a heavenly sign that all would be well. Just like what is shared in Isaiah

26:3, "You will keep in perfect peace those whose minds are steadfast, because they trust in you."

Later that evening, I was reflecting on the conversation and the doctor telling me that Megan probably did not even recognize me as her mother. And with that, I felt myself wallow back up in a sea of self-pity. And in that space the telephone rang, and it was a reporter from a local newspaper following up on Megan's story. During that call, my emotions were still running high, and I let it get the best of me. I found myself venting my frustration about the information shared in the meeting. The reporter was very patient and listened, and questioned, and listened some more. The next day the news article came out, and it was overly critical of the rehab and the insurance company. The article did say I praised the nurses, therapists, and most of the doctors, but not others. I felt awful for the way in which my story came across in this article. I had always tried hard to remain positive to the public and regretted that I had said anything at all. I prayed hard to God to forgive me for the way I shared my feelings.

The article created a lot of stir around the rehab, and I wrote a letter of apology to the staff that night. In hindsight this may have been a vehicle that God used to pick us up and carry us on. God turned a tricky situation, catching the attention of many, and began to receive unsolicited donations for expenses. The article also stimulated a phone call from a home care agency who wanted to meet with us. I initially thought that they wanted to direct us on how to take care of Megan at home. Instead, they guided us to a different type of rehabilitation. They also shared that when the time came, they would help set up our home to care for her. With the wheels in motion to present the insurance company with other options, my friend Lori and I started researching the possibilities. With the hype from the news article, the insurance company made the decision to extend our time at that rehab and would assist us when we made the decision for the next steps. I knew that God provided answers to our prayers. Just like what is shared in Psalm 119:105, "Your word is a lamp for my feet, a light on my path."

My fight to walk in blind faith is sometimes in a full-blown war. Yet with every bump in the road, and the many storms faced, the Lord continues to show me how he is working for the good of many. I remember a time a few years back when the money Megan received from the lawsuit was running out. One of the difficulties of Megan's condition is keeping her body from clenching and becoming rigid, which further limits her mobility. To combat this, we had three dedicated women who each came once a week to give Megan a full body massage and would then bill the bank that managed her account. One day I received notice that this account was now depleted and one of the therapists was not going to be paid. I knew that Megan had just received an increase in her social security, so I was able to reassure all three therapists that we had the money to pay them. I asked the therapist who did not get paid to bring me the bill. I was shocked when she handed me the bill that was for $2,000. She told me that she had been going through some rough times herself that year and billing just got away from her. I knew adding blame to the situation would not help. We were both terribly upset; this was money that I didn't have to give to her, and the tears were flowing from both of us. I then looked up at her and said aloud that when you are feeling hopeless, there is only one thing to do and that is to pray for what we need. I then prayed for God's provision for continued care and for payment of this debt. Within a week, we had a visit from one of our steadfast and loyal donors. This was unusual because he usually sent us a check for $365 each year at Christmas time and it was now summer. During the visit, our friend said he had been thinking of our Megan and then handed an envelope to my husband. When my husband opened the envelope, there was a check for $2,000. The donation was the exact amount that we needed to pay the therapist. As I prayed my thanks to God, I also asked him to keep this friend safe. I was worried that something may be wrong with him since the money was for a large amount and was so unexpected. But leaning into my gratitude, I knew that the Holy Spirit was moving through our friend on that day. I continue to praise the Lord for putting people like this in our path. Recently, this same angel on earth stopped by during the pandemic and left us a bag full of food and placed five $100 bills in the bag with a note of support. I thank God for guiding this friend, along with so many others, for continually bringing heaven to earth for my family.

Another test of me walking blindly in my faith was more recent when I was faced with surgery to remove a tumor that was resting on my brain. Two days before the procedure, Megan became extremely ill, and we had to take her to emergency. It was on a Sunday and the doctor decided to admit her to give her medicine and intense respiratory therapy. In the twenty-three years since Megan's accident, I could count on one hand the times she has been sick. "Why now, Lord?" was my cry. That night my longtime friend called me unexpectedly, we had not talked in weeks, and I began to share my situation. Sure enough, she showed up in Megan's room with Starbucks and a shoulder to cry on. I was told that morning that we would not be going home, and Megan was probably going to be in the hospital for four or five days. What was I going to do—cancel my surgery? Try to get Megan in the hospital where my surgery was going to take place? I was absolutely freaking out. My friend was very worried about me because I was still on the mend from my heart surgery that took place months earlier. My friend encouraged me to take a walk to calm down. I agreed, and just as I got to the threshold of the door, I felt a gentle hand push me back in. I said to my friend, "If I profess to be a woman that 'walks in faith' then I need to trust God to take care of this situation even if I have to walk through it blindly." My husband, who wanted to be with me during my surgery, agreed to stay with Megan during the day. Our wonderful nurse Jonique volunteered to stay during the night with Megan even though she would not get paid. My daughter Kelly found babysitters for my granddaughter so she could remain with me during my surgery and recovery. We all survived our time in the hospital, and as a family, we were reunited back home six days later. The whole experience was a powerful lesson for me to surrender all control to the Maker above and to not lose faith when the storm seems impossible.

Choosing faith is like learning to walk in the dark. When you take the first step in surrendering your will to God, he will reveal the second. He guides us through all of life's happenings and releases us from the shackles that imprison us by fear. Of course, this is always easier said than done, and one of my daily mantras comes from Joshua 1:9, "Be strong and courageous. Do not be afraid; do not be discouraged for the Lord your God will be with you wherever you go." I fully depend on the Lord to be the center of my strength and will continue to do so until I meet him on the other side.

> "8 Let the morning bring me word of your unfailing love, for I have put my trust in you. Show me the way I should go, for to you I entrust my life.
> 9 Rescue me from my enemies, Lord, for I hide myself in you. 10 Teach me to do your will, for you are my God; may your good Spirit lead me on level ground.
>
> (Psalm 143:8-10).

Meditate on God's Truth and Words:

- Capture the message you think God wants you to hear from this chapter.
- Meditation Verse: Read and meditate on the following verse and reflect on how this applies to your everyday life. Pick out one word that stands out most to you when you read the following verse.
    - "Therefore, we do not lose heart. Though outwardly we are wasting away, yet inwardly we are being renewed day by day. For our light and momentary troubles are achieving for us an eternal glory that far outweighs them all. So, we fix our eyes not on what is seen, but on what is unseen, since what is seen is temporary, but what is unseen is eternal." (2 Corinthians 4:16-18)
- Praise Song: Search for the following worship song and listen to it. When you're done, reflect on what you heard and how it made you feel.
    - "Walk By Faith" by Jeremy Camp
- Reflect on the following questions:
    - When have you had to walk with blind faith, and in reflection, how did it turn out?
    - Where have you stumbled on your faith walk?
    - What Scriptures do you rely on to walk with blind faith?

Never Go Hungry with God's Daily Bread

"Then Jesus declared, 'I am the bread of life. Whoever comes to me will never go hungry, and whoever believes in me will never be thirsty.'"
(John 6:35)

I remember the day that I started this book. I was sitting in my makeshift office surrounded by my Bible, journals, and the newspaper clippings from Megan's accident. As I skimmed through my notes, I felt disappointed that the day-to-day details of my life-altering storm were not written down. Instead, my journals were filled with the many scriptures that ministered to me in those terrifying days. As I read though each one, it was so clear to me how God used these verses to nourish and renew my spirit with his word. Through the Lord's holy presence, he reignited my faith and restored my peace. When God called me to share my story, it was never meant to be about the details of the accident, but how the Lord embraced me, never left my side, and provided me with an ever-present comfort.

Divine hope was what we certainly needed when we were at a major crossroad with Megan's care. She had now been at the local rehab facility for several months and the staff had done all that they could do. We were not a family of means and options for the next level rehab she needed was too much to handle on our own. Through my commitment to live by faith and not by sight, I surrendered the next steps to God and fully depended on his grace and mercy. Boy did God show up, and show off, to provide what we needed to move Megan from one level of care to the next. He graciously led us to the knowledge and the means to take her to the Rehabilitation Institute of Chicago and would be under the care of one of the top neurologists in the world. It was an amazing feat, and clearly exemplifies the all-powerful verse from Luke 1:37, "For nothing is impossible with God." The orchestration of happenings was so timely that only God could be the master conductor of the provisions.

The transition of moving Megan from one facility to the next was filled with obstacles. We were emotional, overwhelmed, and the thought of taking those next steps was beyond daunting. One of the first major blocks was the cost of a medical flight to get Megan to Chicago. At the time a one-way ticket was $4,000. Donations were coming in but not at a rate that would secure a flight anytime soon. As the worry began to brew, I spent time one morning reading Scriptures to Megan and praying to God for guidance on whether this was the right decision. I guess the Lord wanted to calm this storm right down because about an hour later, the phone rang from one of Megan's friends from school. The friend went on to explain that she had been holding on to a donation for Megan that was collected from the junior class. This friend expressed regret that she had not brought this donation to us sooner, but she was afraid of how she would react when she saw Megan. We discussed meeting somewhere else if that made her comfortable and she said no that she was now ready for the visit and would stop by later that day.

When Megan's friend appeared at the door, you could tell she was nervous and scared. I silently prayed for God to calm her nerves. Megan, who only showed limited reactions to her environment, turned her head, and smiled when she heard her friend's voice. It immediately comforted our visitor, and she then went on to present us the check from the donations. Now I was figuring it would be a couple hundred dollars at most, but when I opened the envelope, I started to cry and praise God at the same time. I was staring at the amount on the check, it was for exactly $4000.00. Not more, not less, but just what we needed for the medical flight to Chicago. God is perfect in his ways and timing. I explained to this angel at our door that my tears, were tears of joy because she just provided us with the means to fly Megan to her next stage of care. The very next day, we deposited the check into a foundation that had been set for Megan and booked the flight. Praise God, we were going to Chicago!

Now where would I stay? The Chicago facility did not allow for anyone to stay overnight unlike the local rehab center, which I had practically moved in to. I don't remember if it was the same week or the next, but I received a phone call from my niece Kate. My brother had shared with her our next step plans. It just so happened that Kate was in the leasing business and had access to a condo that we could use that was located near the facility. Kate also donated portions of the fees she received for speaking engagements to help pay for the use of the condo during my stay. In addition, her generous and kind in-laws, who I only met once at Kate's wedding, donated additional funds to help support our expenses while we were away. The icing on the cake would be getting to spend time with my beautiful-hearted niece when she would be in Chicago on business. I had been so worried about not being with family and being alone, and God took care of that too.

God's amazing holy spirit continued to flow and embrace us along the way. We received another generous and 'divinely-placed' gift when a father of one of Megan's friends called. He shared a story of how Megan provided a strong presence and support for his daughter during a challenging time. It always warmed my heart to hear stories like this and the positive impact Megan had on others. As there is never a coincidence, the Holy Spirit was working through this family to tend to our needs. The gentleman's wife worked for a major airline, and she donated four tickets that we could use anytime for my family to come to visit us while we were there. God is good all the time and all the time God is good.

God puts many people in our path for many varied reasons, and some helped me to even get even closer to the Lord. People like my prayer warriors, who have proved to me that when two or more people pray together, miracles can happen in the middle. Surrounding myself with people that I can pray with renews my energy and helps to sustain my faith. One group of prayer partners that were truly angels on earth came to Megan while she was in the local rehab during their lunch hour. Together we would pray over Megan. It was such a daily comfort, and I worried that it would be a big loss once I left the center. On the day of the flight, after many prayers and tearful goodbyes, Megan and I bravely boarded a twin-engine Cessna and made our way to Chicago. Once we landed, there was an ambulance waiting for us to transport Megan to the rehab facility. The check-in process was intense and took several hours to get Megan settled into a room. At one point during the wait, Megan fell asleep, and I took that time to get some fresh air. I was flat out spent and could feel myself on the verge of breaking down. As I walked out the front entrance, I bumped right into a couple of women who were praying. They could tell I was distraught and invited me into their prayer circle. I found myself with tears of relief. I just knew that the Holy Spirit helped to shepherd us together. Unbelievably, these women met every weekday at the same time that my prayer circle from the rehab in Rochester met. They invited me to join them whenever I could. Coincidence or God-incidence? Praise be to God for putting so many angels in my path.

Once checked in, I was pleasantly surprised with the room that Megan was assigned to. It had a beautiful view of Lake Michigan and a lovely roommate who had a grandmother-like appeal. As we were getting settled in, I shared with this woman all my fears about not being able to stay with Megan through the night. This sweet woman assured me that she was an exceptionally light sleeper and would keep an ear open. As it turned out she would need to call a nurse on more than one occasion when she noticed Megan in distress. Again, my praise went to God for matching Megan with the perfect roommate to watch over her during the night. I knew this was yet another serving of grace from God. Even though there are times when I feel the pangs of hunger, I know that if I stay in the Lord's presence and accept his daily bread, I will never go hungry. The Lord never promised to shield us from difficulties and hardships, but he does promise to walk with us every step of the way.

One of the factors that made us almost not choose Chicago, was having to leave my family and army of support behind. I just didn't see how I could do this on my own. Family truly is my everything and to my great delight, the Lord also made sure that family was baked into this plan. The donated tickets provided the opportunity for Boz and Kelly to come for a visit the week after we arrived, and my mother-in-law later that same month. In addition, my brother lived in Ohio and planned to drive up for a weekend. The Lord was working hard to keep me connected to the support we needed along the way. Another unexpected gift of family was from my husband's twin cousins, who lived outside of Chicago. I hadn't seen them in more than ten years and about a week after we arrived, I received a call from them, and I was so happy they reached out. I explained where I was staying, and they asked if they could come visit and I readily agreed. We had a wonderful time catching up. They had also brought me some things to make my stay at the Condo more comfortable. They went on to stock the refrigerator and left me a bunch of comfy pillows, throws, puzzles, books and other items to make my space feel like home. After this initial visit, they arranged their schedule to come at least once a week and called frequently to check on me. God's goodness prevailed and provided me the daily bread to feed my soul and deepen my faith.

Through the Lord's Prayer, we are provided the opportunity to pray in a way that will draw us deeper into God's love. When we are in his presence, making it a daily priority, God helps to direct our steps and through the holy spirit brings heaven to earth through the many hands and feet that cross our path. God's daily bread - his grace - helps to transform us from the inside out. I am a witness to God's amazing grace, which has always met me in all situations. And through the ashes of these life storms, the Lord will lift us, and love us, and provides us peace for the journey.

"19 And my God will meet all your needs according to the riches of his glory in Christ Jesus."

(Philippians 4:19)

Meditate on God's Truth and Words:

- Capture the message you think God wants you to hear from this chapter.
- Meditation Verse: Read and meditate on the following verse and reflect on how this applies to your everyday life. Pick out one word that stands out most to you when you read the following verse.
    - 9 So pray this way: Our Father in heaven, may your name be honored,
    - 10 may your kingdom come, may your will be done on earth as it is in heaven.
    - 11 Give us today our daily bread,
    - 12 and forgive us our debts, as we ourselves have forgiven our debtors.
    - 13 And do not lead us into temptation, but deliver us from the evil one. (Matthew 6:9-13)
- Praise Song: Search for the following worship song and listen to it. When you're done, reflect on what you heard and how it made you feel.
    - "Your Grace Finds Me" by Matt Redman
- Reflect on the following questions:
    - How can you use the burdens and challenging times you have walked through to throw a lifeline to someone that may be sinking from a storm?
    - How has the Lord shown up for you in the middle of your storms of life?

Sufficient Grace

"9 But he said to me, "My grace is sufficient for you, for my power is made perfect in weakness." Therefore, I will boast all the more gladly about my weaknesses, so that Christ's power may rest on me."

(2 Corinthians 12:9)

Storms that have swept through my life over the last decades have kept me treading in very deep waters. And if I'm really being honest, I have found myself slipping below the water line on more than one occasion. I try to always lean into the promise the Lord has made us as shared in Isaiah 43:2-12: "When you pass through the waters, I will be with you; and when you pass through the rivers, they will not sweep over you. When you walk through the fire, you will not be burned; the flames will not set you ablaze." But . . . when my circumstances are just too much to bear and my body is physically weak, the devil that's been knocking at my door, just moves right in. The sadness, the depression, the anxieties begin to beat me down. When this happens, I'm so tired and numb. I am unable to focus on anything and just sink deeper into my cesspool of grief. When I get to this place of hopelessness, I know that it is not God forsaking me, but me not being able to connect with him. I know He is there with me, but it's like trying to see him through layers of dense fog. But Jesus left us with the gift of the holy spirit who dwells in all of us. The holy spirit knows what is in our hearts and will take those needs directly to God. Again, our needs are different from our wants, and I have to trust God's will in all situations.

The Lord never promised us a trouble-free life, but he has promised us his sufficient grace in all circumstances. Jesus personally had to walk through the most catastrophic of life storms. He too had moments of weakness when he was in human flesh. In Luke 22:42, Jesus cries out to his Father, "Father, if you are willing, please take this cup of suffering away from me. Yet I want your will to be done, not mine." There are many examples in the Bible of the Lord's disciples facing their own hardships and asking for their suffering to be taken away. In 2Corinthians 12:8-10, Paul pleads repeatedly to the Lord to take the thorns of suffering from him. He tells the Lord he is tired of all the calamities and wants to be relieved from the pain. I can relate to this passage and how Paul is feeling. I too am tired of the constant pains and afflictions that rain down on me and my family. I hate being so beat up, so empty. My stress level is so intense it is making me deaf to God's word.

I want to hear the Lord, not the fear that is screaming in my head. Boz and I are both in various stages of severe health issues and I just don't understand why we have to have so many painful thorns to deal with when we have Megan to care for. I cry out to the Lord, "when is this crown of thorns enough?" The message from Paul reaffirms to me that the persecutions in our lives are used to edify and glorify Gods purpose. He hasn't asked us to do this alone. The Lord promises to go before us, to walk beside us, and to give us the sufficient grace to move through any situation. We just have to trust His plan, and that plan is for good. Being resilient in my faith, no matter the circumstance, is based on my knowledge and experiencing a God that never changes. A God that is not dependent on the strength of my own faith, but the strength of the Lord's faithfulness to me. My crown of thorns has also given me a chance to identify with others who are struggling and to provide love and support that the Lord has shown me. Just as scripture shares in 2 Corinthians 1:3-4, "Praise be to the God and Father of our Lord Jesus Christ, the Father of compassion and the God of all comfort, who comforts us in all our troubles, so that we can comfort those in any trouble with the comfort we ourselves receive from God." Overcoming what can be an overwhelming world is impossible to do without the presence of God, but with his sufficient grace, everything is possible.

Just as we were ready to finish up the editing of this book, life storms were just rolling in. It was a full-blown tsunami. Megan's bed had broken down and was beyond repair. With her bed not rotating, a terrible bed sore had set in. In addition, Boz was getting ready for his third lung surgery. The devil was dancing on our roof. My health was suffering as well, and I was feeling like a doubting Thomas. I once again needed to see that God was with us. The Lord showed up in miraculous ways. The Holy Spirit nudged me to be bold and reach out for help in buying a new bed that now cost forty-six thousand dollars. Within ten days we had most of the money for the bed.

The second miraculous way the Lord showed up was just before Boz's surgery. We were all in a dark storm. But my granddaughter Sophia was not, and we all found ourselves watching her as she was dancing and singing to her favorite Disney movie. When Kelly wheeled Megan into the room, Megan was watching Sophia and started to giggle. Sophia went right up to her and said, "Hi Megan." Megan turned and lifted her head to look at Sophia and said clearly "Hi!" In that moment, Megan was present with us. What a glorious message from God that he was with us.

The servings of grace continued. A few weeks later, Boz made it through his surgery. We were in the post op visit with the oncologist when he shared with us that what he removed was scar tissue and not another tumor. Praise be to God for revealing himself to us in mighty ways. Now I am a realist and I know that Boz will still have trials ahead and that Megan is not going to start talking anytime soon, but God showed us the light of his goodness and his grace is sufficient.

Praising Storms is my personal journey and a true testament of how the Holy Spirit connects me to the power of God. We sow the seeds of faith by sharing our testimonies of His real presence in our lives with others. As we use the gifts God gives us, and say yes to reaching people in his name, powerful things happen. Seeds of faith are planted; lives are changed, and the storms are calmed. As I said before, I know that I am perfectly imperfect, and I pray each day to be still and let God guide me as he pleases. Through the decades of storms, I have mourned many things. I've journeyed through heartaches that are simply indescribable to those without stripes. Yet, following any storm, when the sun comes out, I tend to immediately look up and try to spot a rainbow. I have that laughable confidence that it will be there. And like what is shared in Genesis 9:16, "Whenever I see the rainbow appear in the clouds, I will see it and remember the everlasting covenant between God and all living creatures of every kind on the earth."

"12 We don't yet see things clearly. We're squinting in a fog, peering through a mist. But it won't be long before the weather clears and the sun shines bright! We'll see it all then, see it all as clearly as God sees us, knowing him directly just as he knows us!"

1 Corinthians 13: 12 (Messages)

Megan, Pat, Boz, Kelly and Sophia

Meditate on God's Truth and Words:

Through these chapters, my hope is that you heard the messages that God wants you to hear. As I wrote each chapter, I began to capture what God was revealing and reinforcing in me for this book. These messages are my true witness to God's presence and unstoppable love that help me to praise the storms that cross my path.

- When I call out the Lord's name in full surrender, he is always by my side to calm any storm.
- God wants to be in a relationship with me, which requires my spiritual fitness to stay connected to him and be willing to listen for His messages.
- Through faithful and intentional prayers, my needs and the needs of others are amplified, and circumstances can be transformed.
- Relentless hope is an essential part of me being a believer.
- Each day I have the power to reclaim my joy when I trust in the Lord to provide.
- God is always in the driver's seat, and he puts people in my path, or puts me in the path of others, to prepare and advance his will.
- God is a master weaver and fits everything into a pattern for good.
- When I let go and let God, I harvest a divine peace in my life that transcends all understanding.

- God's grace meets me at my greatest need; his power is made perfect in my weakness.
- The footprints of any life storms remain — we never forget them — but the Lord helps us move from powerless to powerful.
- He helps us to step into our faith and acknowledge that his plan is greater than our individual circumstance.

Acknowledgement

First and foremost, I must acknowledge that it is by God's grace that this book has been completed. His directive to write everything down and be prepared to talk to many is the epitome of this book. I pray that it falls into the hands of those who need to hear of his greatness, loving care, and patience. This is truly just a sampling of the goodness that has been shown to my family during our storms. As the time of serious writing became apparent, so did the trials and my faltering faith.

I must acknowledge the patient endurance, incredible intelligence, and force of nature my niece holds. We have been through the worst storms imaginable both together and individually. Debbie persisted in organizing, researching, reigning me in when needed, and offering encouragement without fail. She added her own knowledge of the goodness of God, and she streamlined our stories so that the book was manageable to read.

I want to thank Megan for her strength and endurance of such a debilitating injury and her quiet encouragement for me to keep going. I love my husband for his willingness to let me go and accomplish this goal. He is used to me being always busy, but this was different. It was an emotional journey that we haven't replayed for many years. He endured my crankiness, sadness, and frustration with myself and things that kept getting in my way of getting this accomplished.

I need to acknowledge and thank Kelly, Megan's sister. Not only did she endure hours of conversation about the book and writing process, but she has also taken physical care of Megan. She has become the protector and advocate for Megan that I had hoped for. Two things a parent worries about with a disabled child—what will happen to my child if I die before them or what will happen to me if my child dies before me? Hard questions to have to deal with, and Kelly has stepped up to take the role of caretaker with either scenario. Although I am relieved to know this, it breaks my heart. Kelly has also given me the blessing of a lifetime, my one and only granddaughter, sweet Sophia.

Family is next to be acknowledged. I grew up with wonderful role models: my mother who lovingly cared for my very ill father, my sister who cared for a child with a severe disability, and many other family members who endured hardships and never gave up. I know God would have provided but by giving me the family that he did, I have always had love, support, laughs, the occasional kick in the pants, and the best "waiting room" crowd one could ask for. I am so appreciative of each of my family members. They love unconditionally and are my biggest cheerleaders.

I want to thank the many people who have been oh so helpful. We wouldn't have survived as well as we did if it were not for you. Close personal friends and strangers that became friends who gave of their time and energy to help with the care of Megan and our family. Throughout the writing of this book, I would like to thank Debbie for her unsurmountable support, fine editing, and ability to keep me on track. We both would like to thank Debbie's Clinton United Methodist Bible Group, my Ladies Bible Study group and an army of prayer warriors and friends that have supported this journey. Our discussions and sharing of God's truths with each other have helped to shape many messages in this book. Debbie and I have been lifted up, prayed for, and encouraged by you all.

Lastly, we would like to thank you, the reader – it was for you who God asked Debbie and I to write about my life storms. Writing about God's loving presence and His guidance through each and every storm is the foundation of faith. I pray that you find God in your storms.

> "But in all these things we overwhelmingly conquer through Him who loved us."
>
> (Romans 8:37 NASB)

Made in the USA
Middletown, DE
01 November 2022